*First paint a big circle for his head
and then a little one for his eye.*

Paint three more circles and colour them in orange.

Now paint his beak.

Fill in the rest of his head in black paint but remember to keep a little white space for his eye.

*Add a flipper, it doesn't matter
if it's not perfect.*

Give him another flipper. Make it nice and long and it will be fine.

(Don't worry if it's messy, paint is always messy!)

Using the thin brush, paint the rest of
his body in orange and give him two flat
orange feet.

Use a little black to make the feet webbed
and give him a yellow eye.

Colour his body using white, yellow and orange.

Now paint his beak orange too.

If you like, choose a colour for your background.

(I've chosen blue like the sea. Penguins love swimming in the sea.)

Add a bit of purple to outline your penguin.
Add some white dots to his flippers and chest.

That's it! you've painted a Penguin...

(now he's ready to go for a swim!)

ASSOCIATED EDITIONS
www.associatededitions.ie

Published by: Associated Editions
33 Melrose Avenue, Dublin 3, Ireland
ISBN 978-1-906-429-17-1
www.associatededitions.ie
© Images: Deborah Donnelly
© Text: Deborah Donnelly,
Anne Brady & Éamonn Hurley 2011.